CH00996868

WRITING ON THE LAKE

an anthology of poetry and prose

WRITING ON THE LAKE

an anthology of poetry and prose

editors
Angela Everitt and Joanna Tasker

Clevedon Community Press

Copyright © the authors and poets

ISBN: 978-0-9935666-0-8

First published 2016 by
Clevedon Community Press
Unit 15, Tweed Road Estate
Clevedon BS21 6RR

LEGAL NOTICE

All rights reserved. No part of this book may be reproduced, stored
in a retrieval system, or transmitted in any form, or by any means,
electronic, mechanical, photocopying, recording,
or otherwise, without prior written permission from Clevedon
Community Bookshop Co-operative Ltd.

Requests to publish works from this book must
be sent to:
Clevedon Community Bookshop Co-operative Ltd.

Editors: Angela Everitt & Joanna Tasker
Copy editor: Guy Johnson
Cover design: Christopher D Jones
Printed and bound by: bookprintinguk

CONTENTS

INTRODUCTION

Angela Everitt and Joanna Tasker

The poetry and prose in this anthology are all inspired by Clevedon Marine Lake on the sea of the Severn Estuary. Our Marine Lake was officially opened on 30 March 1929 and this anthology is published almost to the day, on 2 April 2016, eighty-seven years later, the day of the official launch of the restored Lake. As residents of Clevedon, and editors of this anthology, we record here our sincere appreciation for the work of Marlens, the Marine Lake Enthusiasts Society, a charitable organisation set up to champion the Lake, and for funding from the Heritage Lottery Fund which ensured that necessary renovations could be undertaken in 2015.

Always, the Lake has been significant to those in Clevedon, for long times or short visits. During its early years in the 1930s, it was incredibly popular and became even more so with the addition of changing cubicles, deckchairs, a diving platform and a pavilion. After World War II, the Lake and neighbouring Salthouse Fields flourished with crowded promenades, donkey rides, boats for hire and the miniature railway. Sadly though, during the 1980s, the Lake fell into disuse and decline, with inadequate finances to maintain it. Perhaps the depth of its demise was heralded by a local authority notice put up at the Lake to ban swimming. Local legend has it, however, that the swimmers, who today still swim every day of the year, never gave up. And indeed, the people of Clevedon never truly abandoned the Lake, so much so that *Writing on the Lake* joins in the celebrations of the Lake, now restored, with its ever-growing associated annual celebratory event, the Clevedon Tides Festival.

Clevedon is rich in vibrant community associations who boast Civic Pride, the Clevedon Pier, the Curzon Cinema, as well as the Marine Lake and the Community Bookshop. This anthology is published by the Community Bookshop Co-operative through its newly established Clevedon Community Press. The Co-operative, as well as running its second-hand bookshop, also aims to contribute to the literacy and literary profile of Clevedon. *Writing on the Lake*, a collaborative venture with Marlens, does this so well.

The poetry and prose you will read here provides testimony of the love we, Clevedon residents, visitors, and tourists, feel for the Lake. Here, you will find memories of romances created and broken, and of pranks and adventures of young people, children and grandchildren. Stories are told, in poetry and prose, of true and imagined experiences while dwelling at and swimming in the Lake.

The anthology opens, appropriately, with a piece of prose written by Rita Gregory remembering Millennium Night with her mother. It was just after the war when Joyce Gregory and her daughter Rita were responsible for the management of the Lake and successfully did this for the next thirty years. Rita herself was an extremely successful competitive swimmer and diver undertaking the vast majority of her training in Marine Lake. She won the ladies cup in the Clevedon Long Swim a staggering nineteen times. We hope you enjoy her writing and that too of all her fellow contributors to this anthology, *Writing on the Lake.*

April 2016

MILLENNIUM NIGHT: A MARINE LAKE MEMORY

Rita Gregory

'What are you doing tonight?' asked my mother.

'We're going for a swim,' I replied.

It seemed only appropriate that my mother, one of the original members of Clevedon Amateur Swimming Club, and in charge of bathing at the Lake for many years, should be the last person in the Lake at the end of the old millennium, and the first one in at the beginning of the new.

Setting off with our bathing costumes under our towelling robes, and both with a radio to make sure we were in the Lake on the chimes of Big Ben, we arrived there to the amazement of people on the Point – obviously their special place to celebrate. It even looked as if one young man was about to propose but stopped mid-sentence!

It was a truly memorable night, luckily a very mild one. The sky was alight with fireworks as far as the eye could see, including the entire Welsh coast, along with many huge bonfires – all reflected in the Lake and sea. The tremendous cheers intermingled with the sound of church bells.

We got into the Lake about five minutes to midnight, listened to Big Ben striking the hour, and got out about five minutes later. As it was a warm night, we just put our robes on and walked up to Dial Hill to watch the fireworks, along with many other people.

'I wonder what these people would think if they knew we were stark naked under these robes?' I whispered to my mother.

Truly a very special memory to us, in a very special place.

RESURRECTION LAKE

Bernie Jordan

Cradled beneath a wooded hill,
A sweeping concrete wall of white
Curves around a man-made lake,
Holding the rippling waters tight.

Grey, at times, with wind lashed waves,
Or burning red at end of day,
Dazzling gold in the heat of the sun
Or silvered with moonlight across the bay.

Restored, renewed, brought back to life,
Result of many years' endeavour.
So come, enjoy, walk, swim or sail,
Make sure Marine Lake lasts forever!

MUD, GLORIOUS MUD!

Anonymous

D Day had arrived, that is, Drain the Lake Day, a date in the local calendar hotly anticipated. Crowds jostled along the promenade to see the work begin. Children watched excitedly in pushchairs as parents pointed out diggers and dumpers which had arrived noisily to take part in an engineering solution to a leaky wall. Heavy machinery lined up and parked on the field ready to scrape and remove silt, and knock down and rebuild the crumbling lake structure. Clever folk held forth on the cheapest and most effective ways to finish the job within the allotted time. If only they'd been asked!

Sitting comfortably three storeys up in a luxurious apartment with views to die for, she watched. First thing in the morning with porridge, then lunch, and, if time allowed and there were no outings that day, tea and cake with whoever called by.

It was three weeks later, during a lunchtime sandwich of smoked salmon and freshly picked rocket, that she froze, leaned forward and squinted across the seafront, to try to see why the moaning of machinery and movements of men had halted. Half an hour later a police car parked up out of which stepped two officers. A huddle of hi-viz and police uniforms grabbed the attention of every passerby, some slowed their walks to a snail's pace. Youngsters kicking a can immediately stopped and fiddled on their phones.

Work restarted as usual at 8am the next day. Tractors and diggers were halfway across the Lake now, clearing mud tossed carelessly over the wall during decades of winter storms. Only today it seemed the mud was being put through a second digger and dumper truck before being thrown back to sea and only after being examined closely by two workmen.

The week passed, rain blurred her view. She read continuously as a substitute from watching the wet and windy Lake.

Two days later, another police car arrived. All work stopped again. Plastic bags were handed over. A photographer arrived, snapped away, but was kept at a distance by newly erected fences. More cars pulled up, officials came, stood in circles, decided something and hurriedly left.

Headlines broke that evening on television stations and in local papers. 'Body parts in bags', 'Identity sought' and 'Missing person cases from years gone by to be re-examined'. Theories abounded.

Turning away from the sinking sunset, she looked at the paddle stored along the floor behind the sideboard, and at the helmet collecting dust on a high shelf. A framed photograph on the television of a club, all kitted up, smiling at the person behind the camera, a club president − who went missing one summer's day many years ago.

She looked down now towards her gate. Shiny official cars were parked there. She could count maybe three uniformed officers watching her window, their eyes meeting hers, understanding now on both sides.

Slowly she rose, gathered her coat and bag, and waited for the bell to ring.

WELL MET BY MOONLIGHT

John C Griffiths

'What the 'ell d'you think about on boring nights like this, Ted?' Knocker leant on the low concrete parapet surrounding their gun emplacement staring into the velvety darkness, a Woodbine cupped in the palm of his hand.

'Home, I guess. Me own room, me books. Cycling round the countryside. How 'bout you?' Ted, relaxing beside him, was an unlikely choice of mate for Knocker.

'Gawd, do I miss London,' Knocker said with feeling. 'You can stick this West Country lark. All I think of is getting back there again. Back to me old mates, me old 'aunts. What the 'eck is there to do down 'ere?'

Nothing stirred. It was one of those early summer nights. The Phoney War they called it. War had been declared some months before. Everyone immediately feared a *blitzkrieg*, just like in Spain two or three years previously where the German Luftwaffe had honed their skills, raining death and destruction on those opposing Franco in the Civil War.

There had been several false alarms during this time when, with the rest of the crew, Knocker and Ted would race to man their anti-aircraft guns. Mounted on Poet's Walk above the shore side of Marine Lake, they had an excellent view of the Bristol Channel and, in daylight hours, of South Wales beyond. Not much could be seen at this time of night though – not even a pin prick of light to indicate coastline in the all-enveloping blackout.

Knocker and Ted had quickly become buddies. Called up to the Army at the outbreak of war, they were 'hostilities only', not regulars. Neither had that stoicism that saw regular soldiers through bouts of boredom and inactivity.

Before the war, Knocker, amongst other less salubrious things, had been a tic-tac man on the London dog tracks. As an East Ender from one of London's poorer neighbourhoods, he was streetwise, a tough survivor. He had quickly made his presence felt amongst the rest of the crew who now knew that he was a man to be treated with respect. And in that role, thinking Ted needed looking after, he had taken him under his wing, so to speak. Not just because Ted seemed so obviously out of his depth amongst the lowest military hit men, but also, unlike Knocker, he could read and write. Knocker desperately needed someone he could trust, someone with a sympathetic ear to help keep tabs on his long-term girlfriend back in London.

It looked like it was to become one of those interminable nights of inactivity. Knocker's thoughts began to wander. As he gazed upon the dark stillness of the Lake, his face suddenly lit up.

'Tell you what, Ted,' he said, 'I'll bet you half a crown I can beat you over a length of the Lake.'

'Don't be daft. First of all, Sarge will go mad if he finds us missing; second, we haven't got costumes.' Ted was always the realist.

'What are you then, man or mouse?' Knocker countered. 'Who needs costumes? What 'ave you got to 'ide? We can slip away, never be missed. Won't take long. Come on, for Gawd's sake, let's 'ave a little excitement.'

Ted hesitated but the thought of half a crown was seductive. Worth a couple of pints and a packet of Woodbines. He neglected to tell Knocker that, although he was hopeless at team ball sports, as a youngster he had swum for Surrey schools, and, what's more, had kept it up.

'OK, you're on,' said Ted, and they slipped away in the darkness, descending the long flight of steps to the lower level and the sea wall alongside the Lake. There, they hastily stripped, piled their uniforms against the wall, and lowered themselves into the water as quietly as possible to avoid attracting any attention from the rest of the gun crew. It was much colder than Ted expected but, quickly, the pleasure of being free of prickly sweaty serge clothing more than compensated.

'Right. I'll give the signal to start. We swim the whole length, any stroke, half a crown to the winner,' said Knocker. Ted nodded his agreement.

'Ready, GO!' shouted Knocker, who had already set off before 'ready' was out of his mouth. Ted grinned to himself; he hadn't expected anything else.

It didn't take long for Ted to catch up and surge past Knocker as he raced on, with a powerful crawl, towards the end of the Lake. Nearing the far end, still full of energy, head down in the water, unexpectedly, Ted was brought to an abrupt halt. He had crashed into something or someone – from the feel of soft ample curves and the sound of a high-pitched shriek of alarm, he knew it couldn't possibly be Knocker.

Choking on the water he had just swallowed, suddenly, naked as he was, he became aware of still holding whatever it was in a tight grip while it, she, was doing her very best to escape. Just at that moment Knocker splashed up. 'What the 'eck you got there, Ted, a mermaid?'

Ted was trying desperately to apologise, saying that this wasn't his normal behaviour, when the very thing that he had feared brought an end to any further activity. The air raid siren went off with its distinctive wail. Knocker and Ted clambered out of the water, no time to swim back, and raced along the side of the Lake. No time to stop and get dressed either. Up the steps they dashed, to their positions on the gun, with whistles and taunts of the crew resounding in their ears. Needless to say, it was another false alarm, but this did not save them from a thunderous dressing-down by the Sergeant Major as he had them fall in before him, still in all their glorious nakedness. It would be some time before they would live down that little incident.

A few days later, Ted and Knocker were enjoying a pint in the Salthouse Inn where they were temporarily billeted. They were watching with interest a large group of ATS girls as they enlivened the atmosphere. It had been decided recently that there be a barrage balloon sited on the Salthouse Field to add protection for Bristol and the docks. This was to be operated by squads of these young women, some of them very young, who now were billeted in the homes of local families.

Ted was suddenly aware that one of them had detached herself from the group. She had come to stand beside him and looked at Ted expectantly. In turn, Ted looked blank. Finally she spoke: 'Don't you recognise me? The Lake?'

Ted turned a deep crimson and spluttered, 'Oh Lord, I didn't recognise you with your clothes on.'

Knocker collapsed in helpless laughter.

THERE AND BACK AGAIN

Grace W Hewson

Two pairs of little legs trot beside our own
One hand in his and one in mine
'Just to the Bandstand
    That's enough
        You'll make it —
            Just there and back again.'

Then as they grow, the legs
    can make it to the lake
      to linger there awhile
         before the long way home.

But soon the lake is not the end
Indeed it is the start
    of up the steps and
      past the church
        round the hill
          beyond the Pill
            completing ever growing loops.

Or yet again, we linger by the lake
to watch those growing little legs
    slip into kayak
      or perch athwart a dinghy
        to glide across the silken lake
          safe-shielded from the treacherous sea.

As, now, my own lone legs
      grow weary by the day
           they linger by the lake,
                thoughts wandering wistfully to
                     the churchyard up above.

It is enough
      to glimpse once more
           the sails slip safely by
                Just there and back again.

JANUS

Richard Kefford

The Marine Lake comes into view.

I am transfixed by the beauty of the scene on this frosty January morning. There is no wind, all is calm, not even a wandering zephyr ruffles the surface of the water. A soft white feather seems to float above the surface on a reflection of itself, not daring to enter the unknown world beneath. The bright, white clouds drift slowly across the cerulean sky as their twins swim in the Lake below, an exact inverted image framed by the rocky shore ahead and the concrete bastions differentiate the still water from the rushing tidal estuary beyond.

The clouds move on the water but do not disturb it. Which is real, the clouds in the sky or their inverted reflection in the water? Does it matter? If I took away the picture, by tossing a stone into the Lake, the cloud in the sky would still be there if I looked up; but if the clouds in the sky were moved away by a gentle breeze, the cloud in the water would disappear. It cannot survive alone; it needs its skyborne sibling.

Which am I, the clouds in the sky or the image in the water? Does it matter? Yes, I need to know. Can I exist alone in this universe or do I need something to reflect me into existence?

I cannot stand to think about this, I must sit to contemplate. I slip off my rucksack, enjoying its heft as I swing it off my shoulder. I sit on a rock worn smooth by the passing eons of deep time, waiting and willing to be my seat for a minute fraction of its vast age. It has contributed much to the history of this planet. I respect its seniority.

The encompassing Sunday morning silence wraps itself around me like a blank canvas on an artist's easel. The artist's brush produces small sounds; the sibilant shriek of a seagull, the grunt of a walker's dog; dabs of the brush on the pale background whispering wash of the breakers on the shore.

I decide I cannot survive alone and compose my life mantra.

Just living is not enough, I must have fresh air, freedom, mountains and music.

* * * * *

My feet hurt. It feels like a long walk from the Victorian pier. I forgot my gloves, my hands are cold and stiff.

I look up and see the clouds rolling in. I'll have to hurry as I think my waterproof isn't. Why did we have to come all this way anyway? There is nothing here, no trees, just rocks and concrete. It is so deadly quiet. I should have brought my iPod with perhaps a track or two of Iron Maiden — that would have livened it up a bit.

This Lake we have come to see is just a pond.

'It's only a short walk,' he said.

'The weather looks good,' he said.

'A once-in-a-lifetime experience,' he said.

Never again.

REFLECTIONS

Sally Cornelius

Gazing down to the water's edge in summer reverie,
a small child running breaks free.
Formal suits, berets and bathing suits crowd the promenade,
as in a lost post card.
Gliding by in the flickering light,
a day's outing, mid-summer, bright.
Sail boats drift to the other side,
to greet the intruding incoming tide.
Ripples scatter, images break,
dispersing on the watery lake.
Tide now turned, snaking silently in,
a changing world, on a changing wind.
A child's beret floats
but gone are the old sailing boats.
A new awakening fills the lake.
A dawn, a new day break.

CHUG A CHUG A CHOO CHOO

James Foulds

First it was my children and then my grandchildren. What wonderful memories the Marlens brings back and doubtless will still create in the future. I guess technically it is just the Lake, but, to most of us, it is the whole Saltfield complex.

My own first memory is of my mother-in-law, Ginette, riding in the little train with my two sons. My father-in-law would sit stoically beside her, ensuring that everyone was safe, whilst Ginette waved wildly to anyone who would wave back. Then it was to the swings and an ice cream.

Later, my younger son used to swim in the Lake. He and his friends never worried about the murky water or the muddy bottom. Neither did they care about the temperature. I suppose they were lucky in the water since doubtless there were all sorts of 'dangerous' things lying around. But on a summer's day it was heaven for these lads, a place to work off high spirits and work up an appetite. Buttered bread and chocolate was the usual 'chittery bite'. All these lads are now grown up. But they still talk with fondness of their youth and have passed on their enthusiasm to their children.

My grandchildren love the train. Like their father before them, they can spend hours turning round in circles. Séan, aged nine, has a habit of trying to pick up things as the train goes along whilst being scolded all the time by his responsible eleven-year-old sister.

'You'll fall out.'

'I'm holding on.'

'You'll fall out and get crushed. There'll be blood everywhere!'

So far all seems to have gone safely.

One day, to their extreme disappointment, the train was not running. Long faces and a few tears and sobs.

'Right,' said Mami, their French grandmother, 'Séan take hold of my rucksack and Natalie hold Séan's jacket. Now off we go.'

With that she set off round the empty track shouting, 'Chug a chug a choo choo, chug a chug a choo choo.'

They went the whole way round the track, all three laughing. People looked on in amusement. Grandmothers can be very inventive. The day was saved and the grandchildren still talk with affection about the incident.

Of course, there are other things to do now. The playground is much more sophisticated; the bouncy castle a real highlight. I can still remember Mami launching the two- and three-year-olds through space on to the castle whilst their mother looked on nervously. What's all this about risk assessment? We forget all the mundane safe things we do. It is those with risk that build memories and family myths.

I hope to spend many more days enjoying the Marlens with my family. It is a wonderful space and somewhere of which Clevedon should be proud. In this world of technology we sometimes forget that children have not changed very much. They are still excited by physical challenge. They love creating imaginary worlds. Most of all they love to be part of a historical continuum. That is what the Marlens provides.

'When you were a boy, Daddy, did you come here? Did they have a train then? What did you play at?'

And off they run seeking new adventures.

I LOVE MARINE LAKE!

Guy Johnson

We were perched on the wall of the Lake, feet dangling in the cool water, mulling over whether to go in. It was warm and we always enjoyed it. A child about eight or nine ambled along the wide paving towards us, seemingly distracted and with not much urgent business on his carefree mind. He stopped behind us and asked us if we were going in. We said that we probably were. He sat down and started to take off his shoes and socks, and then his shirt. 'Are you going in?' we asked him, and he said that he was.

And so he lowered himself into the shallow water, sucking in air at the coldness of it, as we always did. Gently finding the stony bottom, he began to swish his way through the water, waist deep, wading and humming to himself, feeling the joy of it all. And then he shot his arms into the air and cried, 'I love Marine Lake!' Such a straightforward expression of truth and enthusiasm! We laughed out loud with him. He was about twenty feet from us.

Then, behind us, appeared a very flustered and anxious mother who had come racing along to find him. He had escaped from her charge, come here, had undressed and got into the water. 'What if you had drowned?' was one of many questions she put to him as he reluctantly made his disappointed way back to the edge of the Lake to join her. She scooped him up and bundled him away, and, as they left, we could hear her cries of alarm fading. She had clearly had a shock.

She hadn't addressed us, or even acknowledged that we had been there. But we had been. We had spoken with the child and told him that we liked the Lake. We had been there when he felt the urge to immerse himself and lower himself carefully into the water. We had been there should he have needed help. But, most of all, we had been there to hear his wonderful heart-felt cry of joy and freedom. It is something that we have never forgotten. Sometimes, when we are swimming, whether in a lake or shallowly in the sea, one of us will suddenly shout out, hands held high with glee, 'I love Marine Lake!'

ESMERALDA

Stephanie Fitch

Donated pink kayak sparked an idea
sketched on a Virgin train trip up north.

Five women friends who make art together,
two rolls of wire netting, one fine mesh, one coarse,
wire cutters, pliers, cramps and leather gloves.

Life-size she appeared as we bent, squeezed and shaped
powerful shoulders to battle the waves,
strong arms to hold tight to the back of her steed.

We wrapped her and strapped her to hold her to form;
we painted and sealed her scales from the storm,
modestly covered the parts which offend.

Curving deliciously her tail held aloft,
hair streaming gold and red in the wind
whilst kayak transformed to a blushing pink fish.

Stream-lined and gallant to forge through the tides,
to swim out together as though they were one.

Six weeks later they were finished and ready to show
this mythical sea creature supported below.

Then followed a week of testing the waters —
roundabouts, lake wall, posing on dry land,
edging slowly, ever closer to the sea.

Her celebratory day, the pontoon in sight,
Esmeralda looks over Marine Lake.
A misty moisty morning, Tides Festival dawns.
Would she be carried upon the bows of a boat?
But gently lowered into icy water,
she floats, perfectly balanced.
Three swimmers smoothly pull her from me.
She blurs in the morning haze
and tear drops.
Strong arms hoist her to the blue island.
A voice bounces eerily out of the mist
'Come on chaps, someone, give her a kiss!'

THE LAKE WAS CLOSED

David Mansfield

I was thirteen to fourteen years of age during the years 1949 and 1950. Often, with my friends, I cycled from home in the Easton district of Bristol to Clevedon. The reason for our trips? We had discovered that the Lake had been closed, but that it was still full of water; even the diving stage had been left in place. We discovered a way in through a broken fence. It never occurred to us there must have been good cause for the closure.

So why visit? Obvious! At that time, the Lake was not subject to any supervision or security. I recall having many hours of free swimming in the water. At its very best, it was incredibly murky. At its worst, it was full of unmentionables. Despite illegal entry, I cannot recall ever being caught or warned off. Our visits, however, eventually were brought to an end by a cat, albeit a dead one.

On this particular occasion we had made our way to Clevedon and as usual made our way through the fence into the Lake. Several of us had jumped into the water, and I decided to jump off the diving stage. I climbed to the top board, and, being given the all-clear by my friends, I ran the length of the board, leapt up and out. My cousin, who had been standing on the side, shouted to me to stop. Too late, I was on my way down. I hit the water and began my ascent to the surface. By this time, several of my friends were standing on the Lake side urging me to get out. A dead cat had appeared floating on the surface of the Lake. Our stirring the water had been sufficient to bring the carcase of the cat to float on the top.

We quickly dressed and made our way home. We were rather disappointed that the cat had seen the end to our free activity.

THE OFF-WORLD SCHOOL EXCURSION

Joan Anderson

Sir drew himself up to his full earth height, one metre sixty centimetres, and raised both arms for silence. He was listing the ground rules which we'd all heard many times before. We hoped he'd be quick, but Sir was seldom speedy. Resigned, we waited.

We were to stay together, not to put anything in our mouths, nor speak to humans — even with our latest-model translator, speech could go horribly wrong. Not to return barks — humans will notice and we mustn't draw attention to ourselves. Not to get on anything with wheels and strictly no souvenirs allowed for health, safety and quarantine reasons.

'We'll all meet in the Salthouse car park, at three, to return to the school outing vehicle. Easy to find, it's next to the newly refurbished Marine Lake. Our vehicle is beautifully disguised to look like a normal school bus. It will be locked until three when it's programmed to open. I'll be keeping an eye on you from the Salthouse terrace.'

'Hey Elasto,' said Kookie. 'Let's explore the sea wall towards the pier.'

'I'm going on the little railway and bouncy castle.'

'Act your age, Elasto. We're too old for those.'

'But we look exactly like these kids,' said Elasto.

'We're not,' said Kookie firmly. 'Maybe later.'

'Ok then,' conceded Elasto as they both headed off in the direction of Clevedon Pier. 'Why do you think humans put their bodies into the lake water? It's cold. We calculated only ten degrees today.'

Kookie explained in a serious voice. 'Sir said they like it, it's very good for bodies, after they have a hot drink.'

'Sir said humans are strange,' mumbled Elasto.

On their way they found the arcade, which hadn't been mentioned in class. Just as one would expect from off-world beings masquerading as schoolboys, this had to be thoroughly investigated. This is a social history trip after all!

'Kookie. We need some of those little coin things to make the machines work.'

'I know and I've got an idea,' said Kookie.

'Kookie, don't you dare,' hissed Elasto.

Kookie eyed up the humans and quietly approached the coin booth. The attendant smiled as he handed over a big bag of coins. Kookie smiled his thanks.

'We are going to get into so much trouble.'

'How? Who's to know?'

'Sir said we are not meant to use telepathy here. It frightens humans,' stated Elasto.

'He's not frightened and already he's forgotten me. I fixed it, don't worry,' said a cheerful Kookie as he led the way towards two spaceship shooting rides where they scored well and were rewarded with a free go.

'Bored,' said Elasto after the second ride. 'Let's go.'

They conned their way onto the pier, the ticket seller thinking they had tickets and were with grown-ups.

'Beat you to the end of the pier,' said Kookie.

They ran at full speed, weaving in and out of humans walking sedately. At the end they sat down to watch humans fishing over the side. They seemed to wait for fish to bite the line. Kookie and Elasto puzzled over why humans would leave so much to chance. A fish, lying in a container, explained. All fish took great trouble to avoid the lines — today he'd been unlucky. Understanding, Elasto gently picked him up and dropped him back into the water while Kookie blocked the fisherman's thoughts so he wouldn't notice. They walked back towards the shore.

Along the sea front towards the Salthouse, they noticed four-legged creatures approaching them, barking.

'I feel rude not answering them. They are just saying hello,' said Elasto.

'I know,' said Kookie. 'Maybe we can just do a very quiet woof so as not to offend.' Both Kookie and Elasto then gave every dog eye contact and a quiet woof. The dogs quickly understood, many giving licks of appreciation. It wasn't every day that they got to meet off-worlders.

Back near Salthouse Fields the boys saw their classmates had all been busy too. One was driving the miniature train. Two were making modifications to a smart phone. Sir would not like that. Six had joined in with a group of human boys to kick a ball around the grass. They'd formed an off-world team versus humans — doing well, too, judging by the groans from the humans. One was riding a donkey, asking the animal not to trip him up. Others had bravely removed their shoes, pulled their shorts up high and were knee-deep paddling in the Lake, shouting at one another. So much for not being noticed! But Kookie's and Elasto's admiration went to two classmates who were fully in the water, had swum to the pontoon and were now loudly declaring it their territory and refusing to let any humans on it.

Easily forgetting their classmates' shenanigans, both Kookie and Elasto were attracted to the food kiosk. Might as well break a few more rules whilst there's time. Humans were putting lots of things into their mouths. A pink fluffy substance on a stick and scoops of something cold which they licked to stop drips down their chins.

'I've still got some coins left,' said Kookie. 'Let's get a few samples. We'll say it's an experiment, a scientific taste test to expand the parameters of our universal history trip.'

'I'll buy that,' said Elasto.

The boys joined the queue and studied the menu board.

'I want some of those pale, little skinny things that smell gorgeous,' said Elasto.

'I think that's fish and chips. It's on the menu. I'm getting a large burger. We could share a double-scoop ice cream.' Kookie paid from the coin bag, working it out quickly from watching humans in the queue before him.

When suitably full up with yummy earth food they noticed their classmates returning towards the school bus. Checking their watches they joined them. Sir was not at the bus waiting for them: everyone was discussing what to do. Kookie and Elasto looked around. They spotted Sir sitting on the Salthouse terrace with a large glass of yellow liquid.

'We'll go and tell him we're all ready.' The class watched as Kookie and Elasto went up onto the terrace. As they drew closer snores told them Sir was asleep with glass in hand. On the glass was the word *Thatchers*. They looked at each other confused. They sniffed the glass and drew back swiftly. It smelt awful.

'We'll get some of the bigger boys to help us get him back to the bus,' said Elasto. 'We can lay him out on the back seat. Do you know how to drive Kookie?'

'Oh yes. My dad warned me once that Sir might fall asleep on the terrace and said I'd best know how to drive.'

'The friendly Salthouse dog said Sir was on his fourth glass and it's normal to be tired drinking Thatchers. He's not going to wake up for a while is he Kookie?'

'OK, everyone, listen,' ordered Kookie. 'Sir is asleep but luckily I can drive the bus. Best sit down with seat belts on. Elasto will do the sat nav and music system. I'll drive us to the Pill where we can engage the cloak and switch to flight mode. Then we fly off over the M5 and M4 to Heathrow where the school ship is cloaked. Then, the school pilots will take over. Enjoy the ride, we'll be home for tea.'

A chorus of agreement. Souvenirs appeared, food stuffed into mouths and the friendly Salthouse dog woofed agreement as he settled down next to Sir.

THE CAPTIVE SEA: A SONNET for the LAKE

Robin Kidson

Break, break, break,
On thy cold grey stones, O Sea!

Alfred, Lord Tennyson

The moon casts its beam on the salty pool,
But can't make these waves dance to its tune;
For we have captured this slice of the sea,
And freed it from its tidal chains;
We've corralled it in the crook of an arm,
Like a child hiding work from prying eyes,
Guarding her pool of salty tears.

We calmed and tamed and broke the sea,
As the cowboy breaks the wildest horse;
It breaks no longer on the cold grey stones,
But laps against the clean concrete,
And gently licks the children's feet;
Strokes the hulls of model ships,
And softly kisses the swimmer's lips.

FLOATING ON THE EDGE

C A Swingler

The seascape took Clare's breath away. She'd not visited her birthplace for many years. During that time, her turbulent, troubled life had eroded her memory of the magical Marine Lake: the wonderful stretch of tidal waters spitting back and forth its cappuccino froth; the elegant Pier as it bravely needles its way into the wash; the hunched trees and majestic sunsets.

As the scene continues to paint itself, she holds a thin pale hand to her forehead to screen the blood-orange setting sun. She watches the bright boats bobbing across the rippling Lake accompanied by a flock of noisy gulls squawking above the lapping waters, looking for a late supper. Their cries drift effortlessly on the soft wind. It's the edge of the world thinks Clare as she drinks in the delicious summer cocktail set out before her.

The sight warms her crumpled lost being like a soft blanket, lifting her spirits and offering a little window through which she can see herself as a young girl, some forty years earlier, dipping her sun-kissed toes into the cool Lake. She hears her mother gently warning her not to get too close to the water. The fresh smell of the Lake touches her senses and innocent laughter fills her memory.

The images flood her sad mind with echoes of happier times before everything changed, before her life began to ebb, like the tide. As Clare anchors her thoughts, she notices the Lake has been restored to its former glory.

She shouts loudly across the Lake. 'Can I be restored?' but no one hears, and her desperate words drag like a heavy fishing net across the water.

As the tide quickly rises, the water licks its way over the rocks, delivering its rolling cargo into the newly cleaned basin. And, like the creeping tide, Clare sees that her life has been running a tidal journey similar to that of the Lake. Sometimes full, bubbling and buoyant; sometimes empty, dark and dangerous. A surge of emotion rises from her chest and salty tears splash onto the sea wall. They quickly dry in the warm air, invisible, like her.

Clare's breath is caught again as the setting sun mirrors a diffused watery light, as though the sun had burst and sprayed its glowing embers onto the Lake. Clare thinks how easy it would be to step into the inviting shimmering Lake to embrace the cool water, and drift out on the tide and over its edge to a new world. Perhaps she would hear her mother's voice again and the sweet sound of laughter.

The gulls have flown, and the boats are dragged from the water by inflated moving shapes. As Clare waits for the closing eye of the sun to complete its showy descent over the Lake, a sliver of thin hope teases her wrecked soul.

A dog barks, a shout is heard, and a stillness floats, in limbo, between day and night, between life and death.

A WOMAN IN A BRIGHT YELLOW RAINCOAT

Philip Arnold

The evening started badly and got worse. Work had been awful. The drive home had added to his gloom, the darkening clouds massing thick. At home he was faced with the familiar dilemma — a beer, food, and feet up in front of the TV, or put on running shoes. Not that he had a choice, what with the half marathon looming. He had to get the miles in.

As he set off, he was surprised at the strength of the wind. Leaving the relative shelter of Marine Parade, he was battered by the north-westerly, grateful though that there was no rain.

The sea was rough, swamping the slipway, and slamming against the sea wall. Spray whipped up over the railings. Passing the amusements, he saw the waves battering the wall of Marine Lake, not yet surging into the ruffled surface of the pool. Salthouse Field was deserted, its green emptiness marred by the pale rectangle, all that remained of the festival stage. Up ahead, the lights of the pub shone brightly. There was no-one else about, except for a woman in a bright yellow raincoat, slowly making her way along the lower promenade.

He climbed up to the wooded path, then rose more steeply up the steps to the look-out. Although sheltered from the wind by the bushes, he could hear the waves smashing against the rocks. Breathing heavily, he eventually reached the turning point, above the boats which were rocking wildly at their moorings. He retraced the path back towards the Lake. As he negotiated the steps down, he glimpsed the woman in the yellow coat, gingerly edging her way onto the sea wall by the sluice. Even as she inched her way along the narrow strip, waves were beginning to flow in a torrent over the decaying concrete.

He shouted over the railings for her to stop, but she was unwilling or unable to hear him above the storm. He ran on towards the steps, calling a warning to a couple making their way to the pub. By the time he made it past the remains of the old diving board, she was at least twenty metres along the wall, motionless, leaning into the gale.

Suddenly she was hit by a blast of wind and water which knocked her back into the Lake. She disappeared and then resurfaced, her coat billowing around her. She was not struggling and her head dipped under. There was nothing else for it. He dived into the dark water, thrashed towards the patch of yellow. He grabbed at the cloth and managed to grip onto her body. She didn't struggle. She seemed to have given up. Maintaining his grip, he backstroked to the relative safety of the wall. By now there were people running down the steps.

Later, as he sat wrapped in a blanket to protect him against the cold, she was stretchered past him. Her eyes fixed on him. She mouthed, 'Why?'

MARINE LAKE MEMORIES

Sylvia Stokes

A figure, gnarled hands, leaning on a stick
watery eyes gaze over the Marine Lake.
Model boats dart to and fro,
controlled from the bank by anxious owners.

Yet in his mind he sees another sight,
a memory of many years gone by.
A boy, grey flannel shorts, scruffy shoes,
running along the side, a stick in hand,
pushing out a sky blue sailing boat.

Young bright eyes look up at an older face,
a stooping figure slightly frail but smiling.
From another generation, watching, waiting
alongside the water of the then new lake.

WILL I? WON'T I?

Jenny Bradley

A slap of salt water at high tide, a wisp of spray, a row of seagulls sit along the seaward wall.

Marine Lake, a mystery of unknown depth, revealed deeper than expected by a lone digger going down and down the drained Lake until dwarfed by mud mountains each side. From four feet to six feet to what? Twelve, twenty?

A big, breezy expanse of marine water, a wind-rippled watery space. Reflections of grey, brown, purple and blue shift across the surface, clouds scud and the weather changes more quickly than the tide.

I itch to explore it in more depth, more intimately, but haven't yet found the courage. A large – an enormous – slightly scary, swimming pool, rescued only by a collection of what look like old blue beer crates floating together as a plastic pontoon too small somehow for the size of the Lake. Maybe there should be two or three, or some buoys, or floating ropes to hang on to.

It looks desolate today as the water laps the edge, wound up by the wind into little troughs and peaks rushing at the edges only to rebound back, rebuffed to crash into each other with a splash.

The concrete is hard, clean, new, under my feet. An icy wind wets my cheeks. I bend, let the water run through my hand, pull it towards me in a small wave. Brown. Cold. And do I have the courage anyway?

A prohibited dog runs, chases a seagull, misses, scampers back to his mistress. She throws a stick skywards in a high arc; the dog's head follows the trajectory. It hunches, then races off, hurling itself at what was an inanimate object, now subject to intense activity and investigation.

The sky is big here, so big you need to turn your head to take it all in. Wales is opposite with a great wedge of wetness between it and the Lake. The water is a different colour. Noticeably different from the estuary. A different texture, scale, a different dimension. Within the Lake, a corner is calmer still. Ringed to shut off power from the people; the miniature motorised remote-controlled boats are concreted safely away from swimmers, paddle-boarders, children in little white-sailed boats.

Transformed by sun. As though someone has put a big smile on its face, the Lake winks and murmurs peacefully, a surreptitious little slurp as the water meets the edge. More people today. No wind.

The reflections are blue; occasional white clouds darken patches of water passing over like a fleeting frown.

A row of children bends over the edge dangling crab lines into the water, peering hopefully at the slightest movement. A row of brightly coloured buckets sits beside them; some heave with previous catches, others are waiting, empty. Bored parents sit smoking, chatting, not watching, backs to the wall. They think they will hear the splash.

I dip my toe in the water. Maybe today?

CROCODILES IN THAT WOOD

Dave Chapple

My father John Chapple left us — my mother Elsie, sisters Marion and Bronwen — sometime in the summer of 1952.

We were living in a flat at 26 Hallam Road, a large Victorian stone residence near the beach. It had been taken over by the Government to house draughtsmen from the Bristol Aeroplane Company.

Draughtsmen, like my father, were considered too valuable to risk being slaughtered by the Lutwaffe when the bombing of the huge Filton BAC plant began in the late autumn of 1940. All of them were moved into Clevedon Hall and to the Walton Park Hotel to carry on with designing Beauforts and Beaufighters.

Elsie and John were both strong swimmers. They first met one summer's day in 1935 when father was playing water polo for Barry at St Fagan's. Elsie showed a strong steady breaststroke off the Pier Beach or at the Marine Lake, while father was a long-swim regular, once coming in third.

After father left us, Elsie took part-time work as a waitress at the Towers Restaurant opposite the pier. This meant a childminder was essential. I don't remember my childminder's name, but I think she may have been a stern and older lady. She lived in a flat around the corner from us in Prince's Road. One dark winter's day, when I was three years old, she took me by the hand, down Hallam Road, into Elton Road and onto the Esplanade. Past that bandstand, past that blasted bent hawthorn, past that double-sided concrete and glass shelter, and onto Salthouse beach, past the Little Harp Café, the Glass Pavilion on the left, and down the steps by the little paddling pool — the start of the Marine Lake.

'Can we go over there?'

'No. There are crocodiles in that wood.'

All I remember was fear. I was a very little boy as I looked from the paddling pool over to the far dark deep end of the Marine Lake. Maybe my minder didn't like her job. Maybe she was tired. Maybe she had to get me back home. And to this day, on visits to Clevedon, I think of those huge murderous childhood monsters, sliding down the steep wooded slope and slinking unseen into dark grey depths.

Making sure that Bronwen and Marion stayed near, the closer I got to swimming, the more I would panic. I was fourteen before I could swim even a short way, and then I hardly went out of my depth. I was never very good, unlike the rest of my family. Treading water was the problem, a sense of inferiority the cause. Father, we were told by Elsie, had played water polo for Barry, and once came third in the Clevedon Long Swim. Elsie loved to swim and breaststroked her way around the Marine Lake, down the Blind Yeo on a hot summer's day and, when there was a warm autumn high tide, off the Pier Beach. Bronwen was pretty good, taking her lead from my elder sister Marion who was a natural.

Both Marion and Bronwen tried hard to overcome my fear of swimming. It soon grew embarrassing for a growing boy to stand useless in the paddling pool. I advanced, if you can call it that, when I thrashed about the shallow part of the main pool close to the cold shower underneath Rita Gregory's hut. Bronwen and Marion would jump off the sea wall, or the top of the diving stage. Or they would swim right out to the raft and back, without a care in the world, while keeping a pitying eye on me, their non-swimming scaredy brother.

I remember the bravest souls diving into the sea, not the Marine Lake, when the spring tides roughed up and over the sea wall to reinvigorate the Lake waters. I remember the pale brown rocks close to the springboard, itself covered in a rough brown sack cloth. I remember the dark water, never very clear at all, from grey to grey-green after a spring tide. I remember, more than once, standing in that paddling pool, or the main Lake, and spotting small green crabs rise slowly to the surface near me and down into the depths again.

I was saved from drowning one August Bank Holiday Monday in 1966 in that brilliant Portishead open-air pool. With confidence inflated by friends and surrounded by pretty girls, able to swim but not to tread water, I jumped in the deep end only to be squashed as I came up by a man jumping off the diving stage. I hit the bottom once, twice, maybe three times. I remember deciding I was in trouble unless I bounced off that eight-foot bottom pretty hard. Third time up, before going down again for perhaps the last time, I was hauled out by a lifeguard. I sat on the edge and he slapped me on the back. Coughing and looking up, in horror and total silence, I saw three hundred pairs of eyes on me. I ran to the shallow end and lost myself among the six-year-olds.

Bronwen and Marion must have heard about this. They re-doubled their mentoring efforts down at the Marine Lake. They told me the salt water would help me float if I tried to tread water out of my depth. I was still useless, still afraid, still an embarrassment to them. Maybe if I had told them of the crocodiles in that wood they might have understood.

They bought me flippers, which were amazing! On quiet days, far away from any other swimmers, I swam out of my depth around the Clevedon Amateur Swimming Club building to the diving stage, and from the sea wall back to the paddling pool wall. Finally, on my own but with my sisters watching, I fast-flippered right over to that mysterious Bali Hai of the Marine Lake, that old wooden raft by the boating lake fence. I was sixteen, and still couldn't tread water. But I made it — scared but exhilarated!

Later, somehow, somewhere, I did become confident to become a swimmer, even in the deep weedy pike-infested waters of the Blind Yeo. But I never did get over that feeling of being left behind, of being scared of something that others close to me found second-nature.

Once, surging out on young flipper-powered legs towards that raft, something big brushed my leg. It might have been a conger eel, lonely, hungry, and tired, waiting for that fresh sea-water surge to take it back to where it belonged in the Bristol Channel.

Crocodiles in that wood, and congers in that Lake — dangers of growing up by the cold grey stony sea!

THE LADY OF THE LAKE

Jenni Jackson

Dusk falls silently,
Creeping over the water
And for that moment
Sky and lake are a freeze frame of mirror images:
Equally azure, calm and still.

The perfect moment
Just as she remembered,
Buried in the distant past,
The beautiful scene;
The unreality of its perfection.

She edges along the boundary wall
Where lake and river meet,
A meeting place of two hearts.
She stops at the sacred spot
And gazes into the never-ending blue.

Time is held in that moment.

The Lady of the Lake

She can almost feel his presence;
Their first kiss captured by
The memory of water,
An image of two lovers
Reflecting through the ripples.

A time-lapse of her life
Plays out in her mind.
With every passing day
She returns to the memory,
Afraid that one day it will sink beyond her grasp.

As sure as day turns to night
The Lady of the Lake is there,
Every dusk without fail
Drowning in her thoughts.

This is her sanctuary,
A place to grieve alone;

The Lady of the Lake

The lake overflows with her tears
And quietens her mind.

But there comes a day
When she returns no more,
The lake is all that is left
To hold their memories deep.

At dusk the path is clear,
A small boy walks to the spot,
Holding his mother tightly
And as they gaze into the liquid blue
New memories float on the surface.

A FRESH START

Corinne Dobinson

New Year's Day. Warm, under the duvet, she checks the weather app.

Cloudy.
4°
Wind ESE.
14mph.
Feels like -1.

Still, got to get out.

She puts on leggings, a skirt and thick socks under her new DMs — actually, pre-owned, half the price and already worn in. Thoughts, unbidden, drop into her mind, conspiring to feed her anxiety. She drives to Clevedon. To Marine Lake perhaps. Now all new and sparkly.

A crowd's gathered there. No parking spaces. Three circuits of Copse Road, The Beach and Alexander Road. Outside the music shop she slams on the brakes. She hopes it's shaken up the driver behind for driving too close. Cars wait while she parks. She feels smug. Everyone wants a space.

She tucks her chin into her polo neck and hunches her shoulders against the wind. She heads for the Lake. Wonders what the fuss is about. Along The Beach a fluttering on the rails catches her eye. She takes a look.

Middle Yeo Surf Life Saving Club
Annual New Year's Day Dip in aid of charity.

She shudders. People are mad. She steps aside to avoid a careering child on a new red scooter. The mother praises the child's progress. She feels invisible. On the shingle below, another parent patiently explains to a toddler the dangers of throwing stones. Pointless while three youths nearby do so with gay abandon.

More people walk towards The Beach than away from it. The carry-on at the Lake must be over. She passes the arcade, feeling less than amused, but finds the aroma of fish and chips comforting. A small, red-cheeked child sits in a toy Ferrari. It smiles gleefully as it glides slowly past, powered by an electric hum. She scowls at the technological alternative to the pedal cars of her own childhood. At least some exercise had been involved.

She arrives at Marine Lake. Now quiet. One family left. Crabbing with a fillet of chicken. The wall above is like a wave about to break, caught in concrete. Flags of the United Nations proudly flap in the wind above its crest. They give the Lake an international air, though rather self-important and somewhat above its station. Health and safety warnings abound, stating the obvious.

Her pace slows on the narrow walkway between the larger and smaller pools. The breeze is gentle here under the wall's protection. She stops. Diagonal ripples run across the Lake's surface, breaking at the water's edge in little waves. The soft lapping blends with the gentle flutter of the flags. With the silence behind, the effect is almost tactile, like stroking skin to soothe. She gazes out across an infinity pool towards Wales. A tug in the estuary moves slowly up river. Gulls line up on the sea wall, heads low, feathers ruffled by the breeze. One raises its wings to catch it and gracefully lifts into the air. Expanse of water, expanse of sky. Space. With that, space to think, space to breathe, space to fly.

WILD LAKE

Pete Dommett

I counted twenty-four of them in total, lined up neatly along the wall that separates the Lake from the sea. Dressed in their dapper black and white garb, they waited and wobbled like dinner-jacketed gentlemen at a taxi rank after a boozy evening do. But this was early morning and they were oystercatchers. Or carrotcatchers, as my youngest son Tom calls them, on account of those bright orange bills. Noisy birds normally: their insistent piping calls carry far across the endless acres of estuary beyond Wain's Hill where they strut and probe for lugworms in the mud. Here, they were hunched and strangely silent.

It was unusual to see them, and so many, by the Lake's edge. But keep your eyes open, and look often enough, and you might chance upon something special. Like a cormorant holding itself in heraldic pose, wet wings stretched out in the sun like ragged, black bunting. And you'll always find gulls, of course: black-headed, black-backed and the more familiar herring gulls. The last of these are the screamers, the roof-top squabblers, the litter-pickers and the chip-nickers.

Once, from the path of Poet's Walk, I saw a gang of gulls chasing another bird inland, mobbing it mercilessly. I had my binoculars with me and could make out a peregrine with a dark lump of prey clutched tightly in its talons. This is what the gulls were after. The falcon dived down to the rocky outcrop by the seaward corner of the Lake, still pursued by the gulls as they tried to hassle it into dropping its quarry. I ran to the Lookout – once used to watch for ships laden with sugar returning from the Caribbean – and scanned the slabs of stone below. Eventually, I found the peregrine, its pebbled grey plumage hard to spot against the background of the boulders, plucking a pigeon and triumphantly casting its feathers to the wind as the gulls looked on jealously.

And it was from these rocks that my children and I watched a man magic-up a monster. He was fishing from this point on a sunny summer morning, while we swam in water the colour of milky tea. As we towelled ourselves dry and waited for the kettle to boil on our spirit stove, his rod arced with the sudden weight of a catch and we shared in the suspense of reeling in a secret from the sea. We weren't prepared for what appeared though: a huge, winged beast tattooed with a leopard's spots. A thornback ray: its name derived from the spiteful barbs running along its spine and tail. The fisherman unhooked it carefully and held it out for us, and some boys in kayaks that had paddled across the Lake, to see. Then he released the fish into the Lake's waters, knowing that the rising tide would soon slip over the wall and sluice it back to its silty seabed home. Still, we didn't go swimming there again for a few days.

WATERY TIDAL GIFT

C A Swingler

A determined salty force
spitting and licking a grey retreat.
Its cappuccino froth foaming,
satisfying the hungry font.

A lake stuck in the shallows
where gulls swoop and squawk.
Shapes shimmer and swell, and
light is sucked into the heavens.

Echoes of times past cast
imagery of sun kissed toes.
A warm pool of laughter,
sails softly on the gentle breeze.

A magic carpet for our pleasure
now restored to reflect its former glory.
A marine lake borrowed and returned,
its watery tidal gift from the sea.

STILL WATERS

Emma Haughton

You could see Marine Lake from my grandparents' house on Dial Hill. The same slate-grey water as the Bristol Channel, its thick stone walls solid-looking and austere. Close up, I liked the way it blended with the sea, like a huge salt-water infinity pool. It was this betwixt-and-between quality of the Lake I found so fascinating. Not sea, nor swimming pool, but with qualities of both. Not exactly natural, nor entirely man-made, retaining something elemental and wild.

It was my favourite destination during my bi-annual visits to Clevedon, one of the first places I would head to on the sea front. In summer, I had plenty of company. The Lake assumed an air of gaiety, a popular destination. In winter, it took on a more forlorn quality. Stark, almost bleak, with a kind of patient endurance. Biding its time, waiting for the crowds to return.

I was particularly fascinated by the ledge that stretched across the western end of the Lake, with its subtle, almost seductive curve. Even today, I can't pass the place without walking its length, peering into the murky water. Always wondering what's down there, on the bottom.

I don't remember ever paddling or swimming in the water, though I suppose I must have done. I can recall my grandmother's warnings about broken glass. I knew it wasn't that deep, yet part of my mind felt the Lake to be fathomless, since you could never see the bottom. Were there ever fish in there? I'm still not sure.

Indeed, it was never entirely clear to me during my childhood what Marine Lake was actually *for*. Swimming? Boating? Fishing? Yet its ambiguity proved an asset when it came to writing my first novel, offering fertile ground for the imagination. In my book, Marine Lake has a strong pull for my characters, much as it had for me as a child. A place which might hold secrets. Somewhere with a faint tinge of menace. Anything could lie beneath that dark water. Even a body.

I was delighted to hear the Lake is being restored, pleased that it will be there to attract and fascinate generations to come. Like the pier, Marine Lake is so much a part of Clevedon. One of its most iconic landmarks. Though I wish I'd been there to see the initial renovations, when the water was first drained. Would have loved to see what actually lay beneath – even if it was no match for my imagination.

MAGIC

Alyson Heap

I was nine years old and I still believed in magic. The beach was my playground during those long summer holidays. I would spend my days rock pooling and combing the shoreline for treasures washed up on the tide. If I was lucky I would see seals bobbing in the channel, their comical whiskers making me laugh out loud. Sometimes I would chat with the anglers who perched on the rocks high above the sea, helping them bait their hooks with fat maggots, watching them cast their lines and feeling their adrenaline when the tug heralded a bite.

My skin was often scorched by the sun and the wind, my knees grazed and my shoes scuffed, but I was healthy, well fed and well loved at home. Best of all I was free, free to roam and explore, and free to watch the sun set, nature's grand finale. My favourite spot to watch this magnificent show was the Marine Lake, newly opened and, for me, the eighth wonder of the world.

This particular evening I sat on the breakwater that surrounded the Lake, my legs dangling off the side, and drank in the colours of the vast sky before me. Here was purple, red, streaks of lavender, all washed across the sky as if an unseen hand had wielded a giant paintbrush. The crimson orb of the sun hung resplendent in the sky, lighting the still water before me with a rosy glow.

I heard her before I saw her, just a soft splash as if a stone had been skimmed across the water, and then a head popped up in front of me and made me scramble to my feet. I saw it was a girl, her long black hair swirling around her,

her head cocked to one side as if weighing up who or what was this person who had intruded on her evening swim.

I said hello but she simply stared at me, and then she was gone, sliding down into the water leaving just a line of delicate bubbles that twinkled in the rays of the setting sun. I waited for her to surface somewhere else in the Lake, but there was no sign of her. My heart began to pound in my chest. I was a competent swimmer and was just about to unhook my sandals in readiness to dive in after her when she leapt up from the water, arms pointed like an arrow, her body stretched, her tail shimmering as she pirouetted across the surface of the Lake.

I held my breath and watched in disbelief as she danced for me. Dipping and swooping, leaping and plunging, the mermaid performed her magic against the backdrop of the setting sun. I laughed and cried as I watched the sheer joy of her performance. She rose up through the water for one final time and, with one great push of her shimmering tail, she disappeared over the sea wall, and was gone.

I never saw her again, although many nights I sat and watched the sun set from the Marine Lake. But I will never forget that a mermaid danced for me.

I am very old but I still believe in magic.

RENAISSANCE

Joan Willcocks

When we were one
we walked beside the lake,
joyous in each other's company.
Then you were here no more
and faith was lost in a
kaleidoscope of sadness.

The lake remained steadfast
in a world bereft of light,
yet I was a stranger to memory.

But time is relentless,
compelling melancholy to retreat
like a sea-fret in the sun
beneath its onslaught.
The lake, rejuvenated, has arisen
resplendent from the ashes.

And so have I.

THE NIGHT

Lubbertus

It was that time of night when nothing moved or ventured out. The last revellers had gone home to sleep off the night, whilst the early workers had not yet stirred. The only light was the full moon, almost directly overhead in a crystal-clear sky. The night was cold and still.

In the middle of the smooth waters of the Lake, bright flashes of light began to appear, as if reflections of the moon's light on tiny waves, or of tiny lights just below the water's surface. The Lake remained perfectly still, only the lights appearing to move. They danced and played as if sending a message back to the moon itself or to something unseen and unimaginable in the sky. Dancing, moving, dimming, brightening, occasionally disappearing altogether, the lights played out their time, then faded gradually, eventually disappearing altogether.

The Lake stayed still and dark and cold for several minutes. However, something was moving. Had anyone been there to witness it they would have had to look very hard to actually see, rather than just perceive, the movement. Right in the very centre of the Lake, almost mathematically precise, the waters began to rise up in a small, but growing bulge. The bulge kept growing as if something was trying to break through to the surface, but never quite able to crack through the surface tension and leap into the cold air. Only there wasn't anything in the water. It was the water itself that was moving.

The bulge grew to several feet across and a couple of feet high, then just stopped dead. Had anyone been looking they would have felt, rather than observed, the bulge of water, not moving but eerily, in some way, appearing to be looking for something. As if to reinforce that feeling, the bulge moved to the edge of the Lake and began moving round the edge, sometimes rising a little, sometimes sinking a little. Was the bulge looking for a way out of the Lake itself perhaps? Who would ever know?

On its return to its starting point, the bulge began a series of straight lines criss-crossing the Lake. For all the world it was as if it was searching for something and, not having found it around the edges of the Lake, was now looking on the bottom of the Lake. All the time the bulge was moving there were absolutely no waves. The only movement was the bulge itself.

As the bulge finished its sweep of the Lake, it returned to its starting point in the very centre, settling there in total calmness. Gradually the bulge began to sink back into the black waters but, as it did, the lights began dancing again, very slowly and dimly at first. As the bulge disappeared completely, the lights danced almost manically for a few seconds, then stopped.

As if to reinforce the now total darkness, the moon disappeared behind a cloud. Total blackness everywhere.

CULTURAL EXCHANGE

Pat and Vivian Stokes

In 1950, Pat, who was then a teenager, went with a group of young people to Hanover on a Bristol-Hanover cultural exchange. Bristol had been badly bombed in the early years of the Second World War and the Allied Forces had flattened Hanover. Pat stayed with the Hampel family: her exchange partner was the daughter, Therasia. At the end of her week in Germany, Herr Hampel indicated that he would like to speak to Pat. They sat either side of the fireplace. He could not speak English but slowly uttered, 'Pat – we are sorry for the war', carefully spoken words she will always remember.

Therasia married and had four children. One of them, Thomas, came to visit us in Clevedon in the summer of 1972. He was fourteen years old and loved his visits to Bristol and London collecting every bus ticket, train ticket, café bill and entry ticket as precious souvenirs to show his family back in Germany.

Every evening we walked down to the front. Thomas liked to sit on a rock at the corner of the boating lake, close to where the swimmers' changing rooms used to be. He would sit for half an hour as the sun set, looking over to the pier, seeing the bandstand and the houses rising towards Dial Hill Road. He was really happy to be there. On his last evening, Thomas was so sad that he was leaving it all behind.

On trailer-tent tours of Europe, we have met up with the families who have sprung from the Hampels who Pat met all those years before. In 1994, Thomas returned to Clevedon with his wife and their two daughters. The days always ended up by the side of the boating lake or down in Ladye Bay.

The cultural exchange played a big part in our lives – recalled every New Year as greeting cards and the latest family photographs arrive.

CLEVEDON BAY

Bernie Jordan

We came at last to the river's mouth
where the banks stood far apart
and a small town nestled on a curving bay,
its beauty warmed my heart.

The tide was high gainst the legs of a Pier,
graceful child of times long gone.
And the waves swept in across three bays
splashed gold by the setting sun.

'That's Clevedon beach, then Little Harp Bay
lies there by the old Bandstand.
And over there is the Salthouse Field.'
We followed his pointing hand.

Lining the shore and climbing the hills,
bright houses faced the breeze
around to the headland where poets once walked
and a church hid among the trees.

The wind took us on round those ancient rocks,
past the boats moored safe in the Pill.
Long I gazed back and I vowed to return
and I did, and I live here still.

A STEP TOO FAR

Corinne Dobinson

Arnold awoke in a cold sweat, like every other day that week. Last Sunday the Vicar had announced excitedly that dredging would start on Marine Lake on Tuesday. Excitement Arnold didn't share.

Since then he'd emerged from his dreams, as if escaping from beneath deep water — breathless, the surface far away. He tried not to dredge up the past, but it would soon be dredged up alright.

The guilt returned. He wondered how he could have done it? *Him*. A retired deputy head. Respected. He volunteered at the bookshop for goodness' sake. Arnold had a tendency towards order and organisation. However, one impulsive, evil act had brought him more suffering than he'd imagined. Not only him.

That evil Thursday, he'd been invited to the headmaster's study. Arnold's study by rights. Arnold was old school. His methods had always worked. He'd said as much at his interview for the head teacher's position. Coveted and long-awaited, natural order had dictated that, upon Mr Brown's retirement, this post should be Arnold's. Yet order had been thrown into chaos upon the appointment of Mr Howard, an outsider. Bitterly aggrieved, Arnold's methods had been set in conflict with Mr Howard's touchy-feely ways. The last straw, the rearrangement of the sports field. Arnold had applied for early retirement.

On 'Evil Thursday' the annoyingly conscientious Mr Howard had refused himself sick leave. Instead he had attended work on strong painkillers for his back. Arnold had anticipated another frustrating discussion, but had found Mr Howard spark out at his desk, one foot resting on a chair. This had fuelled Arnold's pent-up frustration. Acting swiftly, he had seized his opportunity for revenge. Regret had quickly followed. Four weeks later retirement had brought relief, but his celebratory French holiday had felt undeserved.

Now Arnold imagined Mr Howard, wheelchair bound. Would the dredged-up evidence reveal Arnold's identity? He was the only member of staff to have lived in Clevedon. He revisited the scene of the crime, Marine Lake. It calmed his nerves, just as when owning up brings relief. The digger's rhythmical movement was soothing.

Suddenly, a hand slapped on his shoulder. A voice shouted 'Arnold!'. Arnold jumped, feeling he'd been caught red-handed. He turned to face the voice. His legs wobbled.

'How have you been? You haven't been back to see us.'

Arnold's tongue, suddenly dry, prevented speech. *Don't look down. Don't look down.* Arnold couldn't help but look down.

'Your leg...' he blurted hoarsely.

Mr Howard thudded his leg with his walking stick.

'Got it back' he said jovially.

'Sorry?' Arnold whispered, unsure if he was apologising or asking a question.

'My leg' said Mr Howard. 'You remember. It disappeared just before you retired.'

'Oh?' squeezed out Arnold.

'Put an ad in the paper. *Prosthetic leg, Left side. Lost. Reward.* Someone found it in Marine Lake. Pure chance. Dog jumped in, got scared, owner plunged after him and tripped over it. Heaven knows how it got there. It made the papers, but maybe you were away.'

SMALL LAKE MEMORIES

Gerry Small

My earliest memory of the Marine Lake is not a happy one. At least, it wasn't at the time, although over sixty years later it brings a smile to my face.

I must have been about three years old, and was at the Lake expecting to perform my usual one-legged hop around the shallow children's pool, an act which, in my eyes, passed for swimming. But a well-meaning adult, no doubt trying to encourage me to swim properly, had bought me a pair of water wings which I donned enthusiastically before entering the water. Here was the magic device which, without effort on my part, would turn me into a fully fledged swimmer.

For a few seconds I floundered about, and then, catastrophe. To this day I don't know whether I had incorrectly put on the water wings, whether my furious thrashing about had caused them to come loose, or whether they had developed a puncture. Whatever the cause — I sank and emerged with my mouth full of water and in a state of terror. That was, until I realised that I could still bottom it — at which point my fright turned to rage. I stormed out of the pool, ripping the water wings in half in my fury, and screamed, wept and shrieked at all the adults awaiting me on the pool side. I was, as my mother said, in a proper paddy, not least because my *amour propre*, of which I had a great deal at that time, was as punctured as the water wings. And the last straw came when one of my aunts was unable to conceal her mirth at the sight of me in full temper.

I must also have been quite young when, with a deal of nervousness, I witnessed King Neptune propelled on some sort of chariot from the Pier to the Lake. His followers, dressed in weird and wonderful garb, surrounded him except when they were diving into the crowd to grab some unsuspecting (to my eyes, at least) youth or maiden. These prisoners were then marched behind the aquatic monarch and, one by one, joined him on the raft in the Lake. There they were lathered and shaved, men and women, before being propelled from the barber's chair into the Lake where merciless courtiers waited to ensure the victims were thoroughly ducked.

Later years bring happier memories of boats and boatmen. The little paddle boats which I could manage in my pre-teen years, with my sister, taking it in turns to crank around the central Lake. The larger rowing boats in which I gained very meagre competence during my teens. And the fibre-glass boat, the pride of the boatmen, in which they could set out to rescue inept customers in difficulty, or pursue some miscreant child or youth who had failed to respond to the shout of *Come in Number Twenty, your time is up*. One of the boatmen at that time, Bill Cook, had a vocabulary tempered by long years in the navy. His volubility while in hot pursuit would leave Cecil Hillman, who often worked with him, cringing and chuckling.

I remember the occasion when a group of Welshmen on a day trip from a mining village working men's club arrived at the Lake side. They had clearly already had a few drinks, no doubt from the crates of ale that were customarily stowed in the back of those coaches.

'Can we get five in one of those boats?' enquired their spokesman.

'You can try,' said Bill.

Try they would, and were able to push off onto the Lake successfully. However, within a minute the oarsman had proved too inept for the patience of one of his fellows. They both stood up, attempted to change places and over went the boat. Five gentlemen in their Sunday suits floundering about in the water.

'Help, we're drowning!' shouted one of them.

'Stand up, you silly buggers!' shouted Bill.

Eventually they did, and being no more than ten feet from the edge of the Lake, found the water only knee deep. The bedraggled band of would-be mariners climbed out of the Lake and walked mournfully away, to find somewhere to dry off and to be the butt of their comrades' mirth. And no doubt to have a few more drinks to warm themselves up.

And so to my halcyon memories of the Marine Lake. A few summers in the early 1970s when, I remember, the weather was fine for days on end, I would cycle down to the beach to pay Mrs Crow the fee for use of the changing huts, those very basic wooden structures which lined the terrace above the junior pool. Ah, Mrs Crow! How, as teenagers, we worried about getting on the wrong side of you. In retrospect, how important for the operation of the Lake were those long hours you spent there.

By now, in my early twenties, I was less interested in mischief, more in taking a dip, swimming out to the raft and back a few times. Then the periods of sunbathing on the Lake side with other genial regulars of both sexes and all ages, perhaps talking, perhaps reading books, perhaps dozing off mid-sentence. Times too when I would swim out to the raft, clamber on to it, and do my sun bathing there. Times when I would float in the Lake, for minutes on end, just lying back supported by the buoyancy of the salt water and gazing at the blue sky, at the glass shelter above the bowling green with its very convenient clock, at the trees in the grounds of Clevedon Hall in those days St Brandon's School. I made friends in those days, nearly all of them lost now, some dead, others simply taken by the distancing of time. As lost as that beloved raft.

MARINE LAKE – THE VISION

C A Swingler

Marvel at the ebb and flow
A watery tidal gift from the sea
Rolling, brooding, slate grey
Ice-cream white foam spray
Night surfs in on the moon tide
Engraved rivulets rut and grind

Licking salty waters into the font
A lake is born: Tears swell and seep
Kicking fresh life from its moist womb
Embrace the vision, hail the new

FASHION AND ROMANCE

Christine Triffitt

The Marine Lake is looking calm and clear on this beautiful summer's day as I walk along beside it looking out to sea. It is 1930 and the Lake was opened last year much to the delight of locals and visitors alike. I stroll along drinking in the fresh sea air, mingling with those enjoying a day out at the seaside.

I have recently had my long blonde hair cut into a fashionable bob and feel very sophisticated with a sense of freedom and modernity. My hemline comes a few inches below my knees, cream-heeled leather shoes with straps across the instep adorn my feet, and covering my legs are cream rayon stockings. My short-sleeved dress is pale pink cotton with deep pink and green-leaved flowers embroidered on the bodice; it falls straight down to just above the hem where several pleats splay out at the front. I carry a small handbag of soft cream leather, on my hands are dainty cotton cream lace gloves and on my head I wear a felt hat made of pale pink wool which is the height of fashion!

We have agreed to meet by the Marine Lake, Edward and I. I am so excited thinking about him; we haven't known each other long but he always treats me kindly and makes me feel special, so who knows where it may lead? There he is walking towards me looking so jaunty in his summer boater straw hat, a plain white shirt with a blue and white striped tie and a deep blue sweater draped nonchalantly around his broad shoulders, a pair of beige trousers and shiny brown brogue shoes with matching belt completing his look.

He greets me with a big smile on his face and kisses me gently on the cheek. 'What a wonderful day and how lovely you look too,' he says. 'Shall we sit over by the Lake?'

FADED MEMORIES

Zoe Thomas

Day in and day out an elderly female figure sits on a bench at Clevedon seafront. Tourists and locals fear her, whilst others curiously want to know her story. She mutters to herself along with the birds which she feeds.

Wearing a dark overcoat, Evelyn carries nothing but a piece of yellowing crumpled paper. The fountain pen writing on the paper is tall and elongated but joined up like the heads of the waves of a stormy Severn.

A young teenage boy sits next to Evelyn. He does not feel intimidated by the elderly frail woman and offers her a sweet. Her eyes are grey and clouding but a smile comes across her face. In that moment of time, Evelyn is transported back to September 1940.

Snapshots of Kodachrome ghost-like memories fade in. Where was she? Who was she?

[White noise]

Staring out across the Marine Lake, a young girl with a floral dress tied at the waist comes to her mind. The fourth of January 1941 brought with it the invasion of German bombers and the ever-familiar drone of the Heinkel III. Life was for living. From the top of Hill Road, you could see the orange fiery glows of neighbouring cities being bombed by the enemy.

Before the war, Evelyn and her sister used to take the long walk from the top of Poet's Walk past St Andrew's church and down to the Marine Lake, bathing on hot and sunny afternoons.

[Fade to present]

Her heart beat fast, clutching the scrap of paper.

'William?' she said to the boy.

Confusion in older age made it difficult for Evelyn to understand. William was a young Yorkshire soldier based in Clevedon. He met Evelyn whilst visiting the Marine Lake one sunny afternoon.

The boy looked at Evelyn unable to hear her voice. He was not afraid of her. He could see his own dear grandmother in her.

Confusion. The tuning in and out of present and past lives was like an old wireless set. The static and white noise overloading conscious streams of thought, Evelyn began to cry.

'Where is the Lake?' she said aloud.

The Lake was a place of memories, of being with William. They had only just begun courting.

'It is only temporary,' the boy replied.

She remembers seeing the water in the Lake, how sometimes the grey colour of the water would merge into the background of an overcast autumnal day.

'It's gone! He's gone!' Evelyn grew quite distressed and cried.

'The Lake will be back,' said Tom, trying to assuage Evelyn's worries.

She then recited: 'Visit our engraving and hold these memories dearly.'

The lad ran back to his parents who were walking along the seawall. He loved the flags and how they linked the pathway with the woodlands and Poet's Walk. Looking back, the elderly figure has gone.

His fingers find an engraving carved into the tallest oak tree in the woodlands. Could this be their tree? Their engraving?

BY THE LAKE

Eleanor Sargoni

Icy wind
cuts the air
bowing trees
blowing leaves
along paths
where woodland
meets the sea.

Woman stands
wind blown hair
hides her face
that peers at
notice boards.

Thin pink blouse
fishnet tights
short black skirt
creased on thigh
high heels in
frozen grass.

Walkers pass
icy breaths
huddled and
wrapped in coats
gloves and hats

And wonder
where she has
come from so
lightly dressed
this woman
who now stands
in wind that
cuts the air
bowing trees
blowing leaves
along paths
where woodland
meets the sea.

JUST IMAGINE

Bernie Jordan

No fond childhood memories of Marine Lake for me. I grew up in the land-locked Midlands as far from the coast as you can get in England. But I've seen photos taken by Francis Frith and surfed the Net so, even on a grey day with a gusting south-westerly wind blowing rain in my face, even then, I can imagine the scene back in the 1950s.

The whole broad sweep of the paved promenade is covered with bright-striped deck chairs. Adults relax, their faces to the sun or keeping watchful eyes on children splashing and diving in the sparkling water. Shrieks of childish joy mix with screams of seagulls swooping overhead.

Daring lads balance precariously along the narrow retaining wall that makes the Lake possible. The Victorians were the first to build pools for visitors. They would flock to the town on newly built railways or in paddle steamers docked at the Pier, to swim all day, despite the famously high tidal reach of these waters.

Others might stroll on the higher path, breathing deeply the brine fresh air and gazing over the wide sweep of water to mountains of Wales or up-stream to the ferry crossing at Aust, times before the Severn Bridge. Then, turning south to the widening river mouth past the islands of Steep Holm and Flat Holm as they stand guard against invaders, as they have done for centuries.

If I can imagine that as I dwell beside the Lake today, a huge muddy hole that dwarfs digging machines, diving boards and changing rooms long gone, bathing huts, club house, the bathing raft, crowds and the bustle of movement and noise all stilled, if I can imagine that, then surely, surely I can imagine what the future may hold.

What could the Lake be if money were no object? How romantic to have a wide, curving pathway built on the retaining wall so we might walk around the whole perimeter of the Lake. How pleasant to terrace the lower slopes of Poet's Walk so we might sit and admire stunning views. How exciting to restore the changing rooms with showers for swimmers and add a bathing platform out in the Lake, and a splashy area for toddlers, boats for hire and ice-creams for sale. And then, in a recent Clevedon Life magazine, I discovered that this is pretty much the next stage of the plan.

So, full steam ahead! Let's all do our bit to raise funds and see Marine Lake alive with laughter again!

A SUMMER ON THE LAKE

Sylvia Stokes

It was an unusually hot day in the early summer of 1934 when Thomas, a solicitor's clerk, stood looking over Clevedon's Marine Lake. Even though the tide was high there was still a crowd on the promenade enjoying a work-free Sunday. He was watching a cluster of people, most known to him since his school days, dipping in and out of the water and gossiping while sunbathing in deck chairs. It was a time when the young seemed determined to get as much out of life as they could. The Great War, it seemed to them, was long over and there was hope for an everlasting peace. Some were fearful of ominous clouds hanging over Europe, but most tried to ignore these. In the centre of the group he saw a beautiful girl who was certainly getting most of the attention. He could hear laughter bubbling up and he puzzled as to who this vivacious newcomer might be. Getting close, he realized it was Rose Black who had gone away to school when her mother died some years ago. She did seem to be at that school a very long time — most of the rest of the group had left their various educational establishments long ago, but then her father was very bookish, worked in the University he thought.

At that very moment he decided she would be his new conquest, his summer companion. Most of the girls in the group were wary of him now. So many had fallen for his devastating good looks. He had left a string of tears and broken hearts over recent years. He enjoyed the envy of his friends when he entered a room with the prettiest girl on his arm, but he had ambitions and the cost of a wife would certainly get in the way of those.

So that day he started his campaign. He had two main rivals, Richard, a wealthy farmer's son, and John, the son of a successful grocer in Hill Road. At first, he considered these two to be no problem but as the days and then weeks wore on he was surprised that Rose did not immediately fall for his obvious charm. She was happy to go out with him to the cinema or to dances, even take walks along the front, but then she seemed equally pleased to be escorted by Richard or John. This was a new experience for Thomas, but he rose to the challenge.

Richard and John were both smitten by Rose and, after a few weeks, separately decided it was time for her to meet their families. Richard's parents were very pleased with his choice; she looked such a capable girl who would produce a string of healthy offspring to work on the farm. John's father was most impressed by her grasp of business and figures. He thought she would be very useful in the shop. So both sets of parents sat back while they waited for good news. Thomas was not to be left out. For the first time, he took a girl home to meet his mother. She approved of Rose; her intelligence and beauty would help advance Thomas in his career in the law.

Time moved on and summer was coming to its end. Rose had had a wonderful time. All those years cooped up in boarding school and staying with an elderly aunt for most of each holiday had left a great desire for fun at last. She had enjoyed school, was very fond of her father and her aunt, but she felt this summer was to be a kind of reward. It certainly had been. Meanwhile, Thomas was beyond understanding what had gone wrong and decided that desperate steps were needed to remove these persistent rivals. A poster for the fourth annual swimming gala gave him an idea and he quickly searched out Richard and John. He told them that he had talked to Rose and begged her to make her choice between the three of them. 'After a great deal of persuasion,' he had lied, and oh he lied so well, she agreed that she would choose the one who won or was nearest to first in the greasy-pole competition, one of the highlights of the gala. The idea was that challengers balance on a well greased pole and try to knock each other off with sacks full of straw. The boys looked at each other, each convinced that they were the best suited to this task. They certainly thought that Thomas would stand no chance and truly felt a little sorry for him.

Gala day dawned bright and sunny as seemed to be so for many days that summer. Crowds gathered round the Lake and, as the afternoon wore on, the greasy-pole challenge began. Thomas had been eager to help set up the gala the night before. Towards the end of the evening he appeared to have slipped near the edge of the Lake, just saving himself from falling in. It had been quite a dramatic fall. Many rushed forward to help him, but he assured them he was fine. However, the next morning he arrived limping with a stick looking quite sorry for himself — to the delight of his two rivals.

Finally, they were paired in the semi-final. Both had promised Rose they were doing this for her. Their insistence somewhat confused her but, nevertheless, she promised she would be there at the front watching them carefully and, what's more, would give them both a kiss on the cheek for good luck. Now, as they balanced on the pole raising their sacks, Thomas, with no need for a stick, approached Rose and, with a bow, gave her a very pretty posy of flowers. Richard spotted this and John followed his gaze. They both wobbled, wavered and fell into the water simultaneously, an automatic disqualification. The two men climbed out, greasy and a little muddy. Thomas led Rose away so that they could spend the rest of the day and evening together. He was convinced he had won her at last. John and Richard, united in their loss and Thomas' treachery, decided they would give girls a rest for a time and went off to have a pint together.

Rose insisted on going home somewhat early. She gave Thomas a modest kiss good night. She promised he could visit her next morning although warned him she would be gone by eleven. He now knew she was the girl for him and the next morning was up early with an important errand to do before his visit. This took rather longer than he expected, however. As he approached the large Victorian house he could see a car waiting and there was Rose coming out of the front door.

'Oh there you are,' she said. 'I thought we would miss you. It is so sweet of you to turn up to say good bye.'

'Goodbye,' he said looking confused. 'Where are you going?'

'London, to university of course. I'm so excited.'

'University! Girls don't go to university.'

'Of course they do Thomas. Why ever not? Now we must go or we'll miss my train.'

She was in the car waving as her father drove down the road and before Thomas realised what had happened. He waved back feebly and, with his other hand, felt the little box in his pocket. With a heavy heart, he turned round and retraced his steps to the jeweller's shop he had so recently left — indeed a wiser man.

A NEW DAWN

Kate Gay

Suffocated and jumbled, both appealing and appalling,
I'm glad I took the plunge,

Immersing myself in waters rarely clear
but always uplifting,
shielded from the forceful surge,
an oasis of calm.

A place of infinity, harmony and awakening, rising up to
meet surreal cloudscapes and fiery skies, raucous gulls and
potent sea scents.

Where salty lips chat, laugh and gasp, and each warm breath
is stolen by the breeze or doused by silty brine.

Gliding over the embers of a time gone by, bubble webbed
hands and rhythmic feet propel me to the place I feel most
alive.

Re-born, flowing with life.

CLOSE ENCOUNTERS

Robert Bell

The planet was covered in a fog of electromagnetic chatter. The first computerised analysis produced 'oooh ---- babeee -- - ugh!' together with awful thumps, twangs, and gollumps, all in an orderly pattern. They decided to have a closer look and dived into the atmosphere.

'Disgustingly wet,' muttered the pilot at the views shown on the computer screens. 'How could life develop in such a soggy place?'

'Readings show that the surface is 7/8ths liquid,' said the science officer, 'and worse still, $H2O$ heavily tainted with salt.'

'Are you sure?' gasped the leader. 'That's poisonous! Take more readings. Perhaps being of the fourth gender in middle change has affected your judgement.'

'I'll report your ungenderous remarks to the gender council when we return home,' replied the science officer twitching its tails. 'My readings are unaffected by my middle change. See for yourself.'

The leader had to admit the truth and blinked its face-lids in apology.

They'd been voyaging for many turns, had visited 70 planets in 200 solar systems, and were tired of space and of each other. This soggy, poisonous planet was their last call and warranted only a quick visit. They followed a liquid channel for a great distance before hovering invisibly over structures, so symmetrical they might have been artificial.

A huge, upright structure displaying script caught their attention. They floated closer for the computer to analyse it.

BROADCHURCH
SPRING 2013
VISIT SITES

Below these letters were pictures impossible to determine followed by more nonsense letters.

'Evidence of intelligent life or a flag left by aliens?' pondered the leader. They landed in a dry forest and sent a team of five outside, wearing space-suits and carrying weapons, to collect samples. The ground shook and shadows loomed. Before re-entering the ship, a creature, not unlike them, attacked. They killed it, but their weapons set the forest alight. Once inside, as they prepared for take-off, a deluge of water poured over them, dousing the fire. They took off and landed nearby, where another terrible thing happened.

A shadow blotted the outside light as something massive positioned itself above the ship. Then, great lumps of matter buried them. The science officer analysed it.

'It's highly fibrous, organic and chemical.'

'What is it?' asked the leader.

'Poo to you.'

'How dare you insult your leader!'

'Poo falling from the sky? Let's leave immediately!'

'But what if the gender council want us to stay and study it?' asked the pilot. The entire crew went silent at this awful idea.

'Erase the file,' said the leader. 'We were never here. This BROADCHURCH place never existed.'

They took off, determined never to return.

Outside the ship, a Mr Elton reached down to pick up his dog's mess just as it rose up and flew over the sea wall. People said it skipped across the Marine Lake, falling apart in the water. One eagle-eyed boy and a man with binoculars swore they saw a shiny bullet disappear into the sky.

NEW EXPERIENCES

Katherine Howe

As a relative newcomer to Clevedon I have no old memories of the Lake ground but since living here many relatives and friends have enjoyed visiting the area and trying the various activities on offer. My old Mother loved me taking her to the car park (she would never get out of the car!) and be where she could watch children playing on varied equipment provided for them. Of course, at some point during this visit, an ice cream from the little hut would always be requested!

At the other end of the age range, my young grandson has enjoyed the little train and bouncy castle and, at various times, the play equipment increasing his adventurousness as he grew older. He announced prior to a visit one year that he would like to try crabbing. Before they arrived, Granny dutifully bought some equipment from a local shop, one for him (a safer version) and one for Daddy. With great excitement we set out with all the gear, bacon for bait plus an assortment of drinks, eats, a folding chair for me plus some reading material – also for me! Great disappointment as both Daddy and grandson failed to catch any crabs so ultimately Daddy sat in the chair, grandson amused himself doing other things and Granny tried crabbing. Much to the bewilderment of the other two Granny's efforts proved to be very successful.

Older friends have visited and were very keen to swim which they did much to my surprise. I was told the water was cold and the bottom very 'squidgy' underfoot.

Strangely the friend who is notorious for feeling the cold was the one who enjoyed it the most.

Other family members visited on a very cold winter's day. We went for a brisk walk around the ground but the cold won and we retreated to Cadbury garden centre to get warm. They had never been there and I suspect would not wish to go again but the pre-Christmas tat did cause some amusement.

But I think my best memory must be of a visit of friends from Nepal. Hari had been before and he was very anxious for me to meet his new wife, Sarita. Hari explained to me that Sarita had never seen the sea so off we went. I will never forget her face, such utter desolation. I am sure she had a picture in her mind of golden sands and palm trees with blue sea and sky. She was silent for a long time. Eventually Hari and I talked to her but it was clear she didn't understand how it could possibly be like this. But eventually, to my great relief, she cheered up, took off her shoes and socks, sat on a wall and dangled her feet in the water looking perfectly happy and content. I rather suspect, however, that Sarita will never forget her first experience of the sea and neither will I. How wonderful it would have been to possess a magic wand and transform the Lake ground into a tropical island paradise even if only for a few moments!

'MARLENS' - ENDURING CROSS ROADS

James Foulds

The old lake is shiny and still.
Bright children sail colourful dinghies.
Leaking canoes paddle hither and thither.
Pink faced toddlers run shrieking with delight
towards flustered minders eying steep banks and trips.
As grey heads recall long lost memories
new myths are created by the young
and the continuum of life carries on.

Beyond the sea wall
the river laps gently
reaching to a far distant shore
passing Steep Holm and Flat Holm
to the mountains of Wales
with fringes of town
sitting dreamingly in the mist
and pictures engraved on mind's eye.

Warm sun reflects shouts of children
and the drone of an overhead plane.
Elderly walkers stroll joyfully
past young mums pushing prams.
Whilst lovers in their own magic world
stretch out on the embracing grass
disturbed only by the tiny train
and an occasional ball.

This is the domain of the Marlens
where the people of Clevedon meet.
Coffee is drunk at the stand in the fields.
Dripping ice creams consumed all around.
Children have fun as they swing and they jump.
Hearts are exchanged for ever, or
at least for a day.
And the fabric of society is woven.

Writing on the Lake

www.clevedoncommunitybookshop.coop